LIVEN UP THE LEARNING PROCESS!

Knowing how and when to use interactive and engaging training methods is a key ingredient to making learning "stick." *This book is a collection of tried and true activities to get participants engaged and interacting with others to learn something.* There is something here for everyone – accidental trainers and those new to the training field, as well as seasoned trainers. My hope is that you find what you are looking for!

MORE PRAISE

Clearly written, with concrete ideas for application, this book offers sound guidance for people who want to go from performance needs to learning experiences.
-DeAnna C. Myers, Learning and Development Manager, Sargent & Lundy, LLC

Renie combines an engaging, enthusiastic teaching style with deep knowledge of the adult learning process to create a memorable and effective experience for participants. Her practical, hands-on approach is valuable for novice as well as experienced trainers.
-Debbie Groves, Regional Director, KnowledgeAdvis - In

Renie McClay has lived the learning process and provided a guide for professional keep handy. The reader will never disappoi
-Crystal Hyde, CPLP, MA Instructional Designer,

Interactive and Engaging Training – a Practical Guide

Author: Renie McClay, MA, CPLP

Editor: Louann Swedberg

Jacket and Cover Design: Cathy Rabeler

Published by Inspired Learning LLC

www.inspiredtolearn.net

ISBN-10: 1475165447
ISBN-13: 978-1475165449

PRINTED IN THE UNITED STATES OF AMERICA
First Edition

DEDICATION

This book is dedicated to the fabulously talented peers, colleagues and clients I have been blessed to work with over the years. You know who you are. My life is richer because of you.

ADD YOUR IDEAS

Keep the dialogue going!
We would love to hear from you about ideas you have
picked up and how things are working.

Share your own engagement and interaction ideas
with Facebook Group
"Interactive and Engaging Training."
Credit the source as appropriate.

CONTENTS

CHAPTER 1: SETTING THE STAGE

According to adult learning principles, we learn by processing information, linking it to previously held knowledge, and then applying the new information. Being engaged in the process is key for learning to occur. We know learners are more engaged when the training is interactive – meaning that participants are actively working with and responding to the content and each other. So designing your training to include activities and interaction will lead to a more engaging and successful educational program. Let's look at this another way.

SUCCESSFUL TRAINING

What
- Learn something

How
- Take in information
- Link to other knowledge
- Apply to situations

Method
- Activities to engage
- Interactions (with others and content)

Results
- Skills
- Knowledge
- Engagement

The result of a successful training process is acquiring new skills or knowledge. Fun is a natural byproduct of positive engagement during activities and interactions. Let's be clear  here: our goal is *not* to simply have fun during a class (heaven forbid!), rather the goal is to keep learners engaged to maximize their attention and learning. I admit it, I have more fun (both as an instructor and as a participant) if a class is lively. Hmmmm...do you think it's possible that there is actually a valid business reason for leveraging interaction, keeping learners engaged and having fun in a training session?

The focus of this book is to provide a multitude of ways to achieve learning objectives by actively engaging learners and limiting the amount of instructor lecture time. These techniques can be used in any part of the learning event. Many can be used as alternatives to lectures, while others are great ways to engage participation during guided or individual practice. The first part of this book describes the various methods and when to use them. The last section includes exercise examples and easy instructions that can be used to add engagement in the classroom. Some of the interactive methods in this book may be familiar to you, but hopefully some others will be new ideas.

KNOW YOUR AUDIENCE

Before discussing ways to make training more effective (read: engaging) we need to look at some factors to consider when designing activities. One cardinal rule to bear in mind for any event – particularly a learning event – is to know your audience. There are a number of factors that go into understanding your audience. An organization's style, the participants' roles and skill levels, and the skills and abilities of the trainer are elements that need to be considered when designing successful activities. Not all activities will be appropriate in all circumstances. The wrong activity or approach could stymie learning or alienate participants.

ORGANIZATION AND AUDIENCE STYLE

While companies and people don't like to admit it, each organization has a culture and an expected way of doing things. We may want to introduce fun and a variety of activities, but doing so may not be acceptable to the organization or audience. Be cautious and try not to implement too many new activities in a session. We can lighten up training and maintain its effectiveness, but we have to choose our methods wisely.

The key: Seek activities that will nudge participants out of their comfort zones, but take it slow. Design one or two activities that will challenge the "norm" then evaluate how participants respond.

LEARNING STYLES

When it comes to how individuals learn, there are four main styles.

V
A
R
K

VARK is an acronym which identifies the learning styles and how each processes information. The letters stand for:

Visual
Auditory
Read/Write
Kinesthetic

Visual Learners learn by seeing something – a picture or colorful graphic – or visualizing it in their mind. For them, a picture is truly worth a thousand words. Auditory learners learn by hearing information, discussing content and reading aloud. Read/write learners acquire knowledge by reading it then rewriting it in the form of their notes or on flip charts. Kinesthetic learners are those who "learn by doing."

Not until I got into training did I understand this larger learning picture. I found it very interesting to learn about the audio and visual styles and contrast them with my own hands-on (Kinesthetic) learning style. All around me, people were attending lectures and remembering what was taught. This did not work as well for me because listening is not my preferred learning style. Many college and professional classes are not developed with all of the learning styles in mind. As trainers we need to stay inclusive – not focus on one or two learning styles but rather, include them all.

The key: An activity will solidify the learning for all learning styles.

So far we reviewed several important factors that impact learning. Next, let's look at some ideas to change things up – to make them engaging.

CHAPTER 2: LIVENING UP THE LEARNING PROCESS

Now that we have discussed why it is important to include interaction and engage participants in your training, as well as some of the points to consider about your audience when designing training, let's turn to specific activities you can incorporate into your program.

Training events typically involve a few basic steps. The information is shared, it is shown in action, and then participants have a chance to try it themselves. A common shorthand reference for this approach is **tell, show, do**.

Mike Rockelmann, contributor to *Fortify Your Sales Force* and *The Essential Guide to Training Global Audiences*, suggests a slight variation on the simple learning process mentioned above. He suggests learning has these steps:

High Level Learning Steps

1. Introduction to material
2. Guided practice
3. Individual practice

The last two steps involving practice tend to be more interactive and include the application of the knowledge and skills. Because it's easier to incorporate engaging activities in learning that involves practice, we will focus on the first step - offering ideas to make the introduction to  the material more fun and interactive. Later in the book, I will also offer some ideas on how to vary the methods of practice, but first things first.

An introduction to material does not have to be a one-way communication from the instructor to the learner, as many people believe. The idea that participants cannot learn unless new information is first explained to them is fundamentally wrong. People acquire new knowledge and skills every day, and they do so through their own research and experience.

Think about the first time you used Word or Excel, or even the last time you purchased a new car or used a DVD player. How did you learn to use these tools? Did you attend a class? Probably not. We learn by trial and error, or by using resources such as manuals, the Internet, relatives or friends, and help menus. Because we had a reason to learn how to use these tools, we were engaged in the process, and as a result, the lessons tend to stay with us. This is how we should approach training classes and meetings.

The key: People are capable; they learn new skills and achieve their goals every day. It's a mistake to sell them short in the classroom.

When introducing material in a class, don't just create a single interactive way to share the information. Choose a technique or two that is relevant to the content and present it in a way that will enable this information to be used back on the job. Consider the application of knowledge in your approach to be creative in presenting the material. Instead of presenting, perhaps you can have your learners apply their new found knowledge so it sticks with them.

The key: To make your training more effective and engaging, use a variety of techniques to introduce learners to the material.

Let's take a look at several interactive ways to introduce material.

LIMIT LECTURES

Before we go any further, drop any preconceived ideas that a lecture is needed at some point during the program. It's true the instructor may need to provide information, but there are times you can do so without the use of any lecture. Be creative; lecturing is not the only way.

Mike Rockelmann shared an example that really drives home the point that there are alternatives to lectures. It involved training for a product labeling and marketing group at a major pharmaceutical company. The course was one in a three-day-long program designed to teach the FDA laws and regulations relating to the labeling and marketing of drug products. It was one of the lowest-evaluated courses in the program. The original course was designed and delivered by a vice president within the group and had a three-hour lecture with 150 PowerPoint slides. Mike convinced the vice president to try a new method and allow him to co-facilitate the course. Here's what the new course outline looked like.

Revised Course Agenda

15 minutes	Overview of the course, learning objectives, and why it is important.
30 minutes	Divide the class into three groups.
	Hand out the laws and regulations, drug label and marketing material to each group. Groups identify where and how the laws and regulation were applied in the drug label.
30 minutes	Groups present findings and discuss laws and regulations.
15 minutes	Instructor reviews laws, regulations, and major learning points.
30 minutes	Groups take a hypothetical drug and create a label and regulations. Points are awarded for the best materials that follow all rules.
45 minutes	Groups present their label and marketing materials.
	Instructors rate the material.
15 minutes	Review of key learnings and questions.

Notice that the class involved no lecture or instructor-focused activities. Almost all of the learning was completed and presented by the participants. Even without the lecture, the key objectives of having a technique to identify laws and regulations as they relate to drug labeling were achieved. The elements of the class—including activities, teamwork, real-life scenarios, research, competition, and a theme—were included. The

 trainer could have lectured on laws and regulations and drug labeling, and how to link the two, but instead used social and fun activities that had participants applying the information at every step. Participants remembered these activities and how they created the answers when they returned to their jobs. Oh, and by the way, after the new format was implemented, the evaluation rating rose dramatically - it became one of the most fun and effective courses offered.

Use this example as a starting point when considering the kinds of methodologies you can incorporate into your program. It is meant to open your thinking and increase your receptivity to a new way of training that works. While lectures or variations of lectures may be needed at different points, you should also trust that the participants are capable of learning on their own and that they can draw the main learning points from materials just as well as the instructor can. In fact, having participants draw out the learning points and then having the instructor review them is more effective because the participants have created the information for themselves instead of passively receiving it.

The key: Trust that your audience can lead learning and can do so without lectures.

Kimberly Seeger, author of *111 Questions to Design Learning*, suggests there are 10 Ways to Lose Your Learner.

1. **Start with a lengthy introduction of yourself.** Learner's brains are curious about what they will learn and how they can apply it to their situations. Who you are as a trainer and all of your credentials is not relevant to the learning.
   Suggest: Include a bio in the learning materials or provide prior to the learning session

2. **Waste time talking about breaks, restrooms, etc.** Time is the most valuable resource for learners. How can you best use every minute to help them learn, practice and apply?

Suggest: Post signs or provide a printed guide with a map, agenda and other logistical information.

3. **Ignore what learners need**. Malcolm Knowles' research indicates that adults are problem-centered. They learn to solve problems therefore we must create learning experiences that respond to a specific need. Also known as What's In It For Me? (WIIFM)
Suggest: Facilitate problem solving activities whereby learners can apply new knowledge and skills to current issues.

4. **Talk (LECTURE) longer than 8 minutes.** The ability to listen with attention is less than 8 minutes for adults. We have been programmed for commercials and a change of pace by our external environment.
Suggest: Lecture if you must, but build in interaction or activities at least every 8 minutes.

5. **Be the "sage on the stage."** There are some experts who use the learning environment as their platform to demonstrate their own skills or knowledge. They will tell long, detailed stories about an experience

that does not support learning. Is your goal to impress or help people learn?

Suggest: Offer to answer questions about your experiences on an individual basis and when the situation warrants. Limit stories to the specific learning points.

6. **Have disorganized content (no chunking).** Random information cannot be sorted and organized in a learner's brain without some assistance.

 Suggest: Group content in smaller, consumable units with clear separation between topics.

7. **Play games with no relevance or purpose.** Playing games with no relevance to the topic is a time waster.

 Suggest: Design interactive activities which connect learners to each other AND the content.

8. **Show slides, slides and more slides.** Too many slides and reading the words from the screen causes disengagement.

 Suggest: Offer visuals to support and illustrate key points.

9. **Print the slides as the workbook.** Your slides are visual support, not a self-directed learning tool.

 Suggest: Provide learners with only the materials to reinforce key points, elaborate on data or outline additional learning resources.

10. **Stand or sit in the front of the room with no movement.** Learners need to form a relationship with the facilitator to feel safe and be eager to learn.

Suggest: Use your body to grow relationships and create energy in the learning environment.

Now let's look at some other alternatives to lectures and activities that can be used in your training program.

LECTURES THAT DON'T LOOK LIKE LECTURES

Sometimes you need to present content, because it just doesn't lend itself to a fun little game. Some of the following activities are still instructor-led, but they offer interaction so that participants must think instead of being passive learners. They can be used in the place of lectures, or to support a lecture. What follows is a high level overview of these techniques. Additional detail about how to structure these and some sample scripts are provided later in the book.

 *Expert panel* (see Resources section at the end of this book for a sample agenda). Have knowledgeable people come in to discuss the topic. They can answer questions and offer different

viewpoints. When should you use this? Some examples include when entering a new industry or market segment; using executives to talk during new employee Onboarding; having product management present during a new product rollout.

Use the Socratic Method to draw the information out of the group. That is, question the participants and use their answers to your questions as the basis for asking another question. The idea is to lead the participants to the point you're trying to make, and to make them think things through. They apply the information for themselves, linking it to previous knowledge as you lead the discussion with questions.

Do a "chalk talk." Diagram the process or a concept in such a way that the listeners are following the evolution of the concept visually as well as hearing it. For an extra twist, have several participants come up and each (or collectively) draw out the diagram as you discuss the concept. It's very interesting to see what participants envision when something is described for them.

Audio or video. A video is really in the same category as a lecture because of the lack of interaction. Years ago, videos were frequently used to open or close a session. An Olympic athlete or a successful coach would talk about motivation - that all you have to do is want it bad enough and work hard and you'll achieve it. It had nothing to do with the content, but it was flashy and made us feel good. Companies are trying to find a more direct tie to content, theme, or audience for videos these days. And today's videos are closer to 5 minutes than they are to the 20-minute (or longer) videos of long ago.

It's possible to use a recorded situation to present a topic or idea, and make it more engaging and interactive by stopping it regularly for discussion. The audio portion is still similar to lecture, but the format is different by interspersing participation from the group. This technique should not be overdone because it quickly gets monotonous. It can be done with flair that is often difficult to do in a live training environment. To increase interest of the video or audio portion, develop recordings to look or sound like a newscast or an interview. Involve personalities from the organization (leaders, management, or team members) to increase interest.

Refer back to pre-reading and have a question and answer period. Any of the exercises listed in the next sections (review game, group teaching, role plays, case studies, etc.) can be used to assess understanding and then be followed by a discussion to clarify material.

Put an idea on trial. (See the Resource section at the end of this book for an example script.) This activity presents and explores an idea in a structured way that most people will be familiar with through television and movies, if not by firsthand experience. Using a judge, prosecutor, and defense attorney, you will examine both sides of an issue. This works well as a review of the previous day's content. (Learners can pour over the salient point while preparing for the trial.)

Debate. Two individuals (or teams) each take one side of an issue and present to the group in the form of a formal debate. After the debate is over, a conclusion is made about the topic or issue. This is a fun way to present ideas, but it can get long. Consider limiting the cross-examination to one or two questions, and giving a time limit to each side. The first time you do it, try to keep it to 20 or 30 minutes. If people are into the roles, and they often are, it can go pretty long. I love using people from the class audience for roles like these whenever possible. (See the Resource section at the end of this book for an example outline.)

Watch out: If there is a predetermined outcome, do not use this method. This method helps identify and bring out points from both sides. If there is a single clearly right answer, it is best to just present the right answer.

REVIEW GAMES

You can start your program with a question-and-answer game or use it as a conclusion or review. Reviews can be a great way to begin a module if you believe the participants have a base knowledge of the topic. It acts like a pretest in which you can then discuss each point and offer more information to correct misconceptions or fill information gaps. Do not use such activities if the participants cannot provide any answers, as it will de-motivate them. Review games at the end of a session can be an effective way to test understanding and increase energy.

Board games and TV shows. Any game that we have played or seen on TV—*Who Wants to be a Millionaire, Jeopardy, Trivial Pursuit,* card games, or even *Chutes and Ladders* or *Candy Land* —can be the model for this activity. It can be presented in a low tech way, such as using a board from an actual game  with customized questions. A higher tech approach can use PowerPoint or software programs such as Gameshow Pro (can be purchased at *www.learningware.com*). Plain board games can be purchased from companies like Trainer's Warehouse (*www.trainerswarehouse.com*) and customized for your own theme.

Card games. How many ways can you split up a topic? How much can be learned by putting things back together again that have been split up? "Shuffling a deck" of mixed items that were once together is a simple process to create and use that can reinforce lessons on processes or important combinations of elements. (More in the Resource section.)

Historical timeline. A variation of a card game is to use cards to put information in a time sequence. I have used this to discuss company history in new-hire orientations. Give new hires prework that includes a summary of the company history to read before they come to class. Put posters on the wall with decades written at the top (you can also do this online). Make cards with the historical facts of the company, with no reference to dates.

Distribute the shuffled cards between the participants. First have each individual put their card(s) on the decade poster (or decade timeline) where they think it belongs. Next, have the group look at the results. Let them discuss and, as a team, arrange the cards to represent the correct history, as they remember it. Finally, give them a summary of the history, written in paragraph form. Let the group make any corrections that are needed. When all the cards are in the right place, have the group summarize each decade for the company history. This can be an entirely learner-directed process and is an alternative to a death by PowerPoint presentation that reviews the company history. See the Resource section at the end of this book for an example.

Game or review questions can be straight product facts, key benefits, or customer problems/scenarios. Keep the information relevant to the topic. If you have the budget, you can incorporate an audience response system to track how learners are doing. Review games work very well to reinforce product information and other factual information.

GROUP TEACHING

Group teaching is another method that can be used in place of a lecture, or afterward to help participants apply knowledge or see its application. If used in place of a lecture, provide the needed materials to the group that will teach the lesson, including guidelines on use of flip charts or an activity to help teach. Assign teams to research the topics and present them to the group. As the facilitator, add only critical items that were overlooked. My rule is that the whole team goes up front to present, even if they don't all have speaking parts.

This method works well when discussing competitors or products. Each team can research one topic using brochures, Internet, product samples reviews and other generally available materials. They can compare product lines, quality, and sales forces, or identify strengths and weaknesses. You can also incorporate QR codes for teams to use as source content.

If testing or exams are involved, give groups time to make their own flash cards. Digesting the content enough to write the questions on the flash card helps solidify the learning.

One thing I love about this is the physical movement. Participants can do this anywhere, and will often end up on the floor with a laptop or a flip chart. I love activities that move people out of their seats and into different places. This keeps the energy level up and the participants engaged.

LEVERAGING TECHNOLOGY

There are so many ways to leverage technology in the classroom that were not possible even several years ago. One of those is Twitter. Using a Twitter

backchannel engages your participants by allowing them to capture notes and key points from your presentation. It can be a way to poll your audience and gain feedback (using a unique #hashtag identifier). Asking participants to use Twitter, knowing that there will be times in which you will be monitoring the back channel, encourages participation.

Trish Uhl, contributor to *Fortify Your Sales Force* and *10 Steps to Successful Teams* and technology maven, offers some suggestions of how to use technology to add interaction to a classroom setting:

- General availability of cool tools at lower price points means we can now easily and cheaply deliver instruction using a variety of media. For example, we know it takes people interacting with information multiple times in multiple ways to learn. Now we can more easily accelerate that process - e.g. deliver a lecture, watch a video, conduct a group debrief, collect feedback.
- Establish two-way dialogue. One way to do this is by gaining immediate feedback from the audience. This can be when they are in the room

with us (e.g. thru polling devices) or not (using online polling devices, Twitter, EverNote, etc). We can adjust our facilitation and content to meet the specific needs of an audience in (as Bob Mosher would say!) their moment of need.

- Personalize learning. Participants now have options. People can self-select the activities they do because (again) it's easy and cheap to create and deliver skills practice and content in multiple formats. For example, learning vocabulary terms - I can offer audio files/podcasts that some students elect to listen to; others may want to learn the words and definitions via word puzzles - like crosswords.

- Tailor our facilitation to suit the needs of individuals. For example, we can give people assignments to complete in tech-based environments where performance is tracked and reports are sent to the facilitator offering specific feedback on a participant by participant basis. Facilitators can use this visibility into individual need to offer individual and direct interventions. (It also allows us to more easily test our tests and skills audit. We can collect trending information. For example, if 90% of our students get Answer X wrong and do not properly complete Assignment Y – how do we need to adjust/correct?)

- Automate communications between courses, classes, and assignments. For example, let's say I'm teaching a 10-week course and I want to send weekly tips and reminders to participants to help motivate them through support, encouragement and increased communication. I can set those messages up and leave it to the technology to send them out, as per the schedule I set.
- Allow participants to be adventurous in their communication methods back. I can ask participants to complete an assignment and create a deliverable that suits them - e.g. one person might send in an audio file; another a video; another a Word doc, etc. So not only do we, as facilitators, have flexibility in our outputs, we can offer participants flexible options as well.

Other ways to leverage technology tools in the learning process:
- Create a LinkedIn or Facebook Group (can be private) for learners to stay in touch and contribute ideas after the learning event.
- Use Social Bookmarking as an electronic bibliography (www.delicious.com, www.diigo.com).
- Create an online repository of supporting audio, video, urls, files, photos using a WIKI (www.wikiworks.com) or Blog. (You can create a

blog at blogger.com in about 15 minutes. Have one that is course specific.)

- Use a photo site like Pinterest for people to add photos representing their culture. This can be used in classroom introductions, for a new team getting together or for a virtual team to get to know each other better. People can post photos of themselves, something representing their culture, their favorite food, their favorite place, etc.

- Have small groups record their activity (role play or new process or skit to demonstrate a concept) with their phone and post to a private channel on YouTube. Then share all or snippets with the class.

- Add a polling question to a slide (www.polleverywhere.com is free for small audiences).

There can be an advantage to distract people from personal use of phones in the classroom by using those very phones to keep their attention. Using QR Codes in training and presentations are a great way to interact with your participants and engage them using technology and tools they are already using.

Larry Straining, author of *111 Creative Ways to Use QR Codes*, shares examples of ways to engage your participants in your presentations.

- Use QR Codes to take participants directly to Level 1 Evaluations.
- Use a sheet of QR Codes that link to your activities. Have participants scan the appropriate code when it is time to complete that task or activity during your session.
- Use a QR Code to link to materials participants will need for each section of training.
- Provide QR Code links to videos for review after your session is over for performance support.
- Add a QR Code to your promotional documents that links to videos of participants providing feedback from your sessions.
- Assume not everyone is going to have a smart phone; use QR Codes as an opportunity to form teams. Each team should have at least one person with a technology enabled device. It can also introduce people to new technology.
- Add links to the presenter's contact pages at the beginning and end of a presentation.
- When citing statistics or other reference material, add a QR Code that takes participants directly to the source article.
- Include a QR Code in your slide decks that allows participants to download your presentation.
- Use a QR Code to take participants to a survey during a presentation.

- Add a QR Code to your marketing pieces that provides a video of you promoting your session.
- Place a QR Code on your speaking proposals with a link to a sample video of you presenting.

Be sure to review your content and know your audience before you select an approach to use. If you are using a new tool, practice and practice it before you are in front of a group or before you send out instructions. Also, when using new methods or tools, be ready to adjust along the way. If an activity is not going well, intervene by giving hints or reviewing the goals or outcome of the activity.

CHAPTER 3: GEARING UP GUIDED AND INDIVIDUAL PRACTICE

Several of the alternates to lectures mentioned previously can also be used for the learning process steps of guided and individual practice. Review games and group teaching are examples of non-lecture methods that increase interactivity and fun at any step in the learning process. The methods that follow lend themselves to techniques for practicing skills.

SCAVENGER HUNTS

Ever go on a scavenger hunt as a kid, walking through the neighborhood looking for a paper clip, a cinnamon stick, yesterday's newspaper? Looking for things is a great way to get to know resources. A scavenger hunt on a company intranet or in a corporate headquarters is a good way for people to start learning their way around and discovering where to find things. You can send the group out to evaluate sales techniques at stores, in the hotel shops, or that night at dinner. Many companies use this method to check out competition, or to look at retail products. The key is to provide a list of items to locate or observe based on the program's learning objectives and content. It is interesting to have participants come back and present their findings to the class and include any interesting anecdotes. See Additional Resources at the end of the book for specific examples of scavenger hunts in a corporate headquarters and on an intranet.

CASE STUDIES

Case studies are a widely used and effective way to teach key concepts and skills, and can be used anytime in a session. Case studies at the beginning of a session can create interest in the topic and offer a way to judge the knowledge of participants. After presenting a case study, you can then offer participants a new way to think about the situation, and then have them apply the new model or way of thinking to the case study and see the difference. This helps link a new way of thinking to an old process.

Case studies are effective because they bring in real-life. They also take the learning to a higher level because participants need to understand and apply the knowledge.

Case Study Benefits

- Promote thinking
- Are largely a participant-directed training methodology
- Are generally nonthreatening to participants (check for culture acceptance)
- Build on the experiences of the learner
- Let people see the issues
- Are cost-effective because you can write it once and use it over and over
- Can be customized to the organization's needs; can have different versions for different divisions or job levels, if needed

There are some disadvantages to case studies as well. While a lecture may require minimal preparation, writing case studies takes certain skills and some time to be done well. They are also more time-consuming to run. The learning is often greater, but sometimes available class or development time is a factor. Case studies can also take participants off the intended learning path if they begin to argue about the details or how to interpret the case.

Use a Case Study for These Reasons

- Practice a newly learned skill or putting together everything that has been learned during a workshop
- Progressively add more complex information to a situation
- Problem solving

A variation of the case study, a shorter scenario, can be used to open a session, can be used for skill building, or can be a closing exercise.

ROLE PLAY

Role playing is a tried-and-true method and it is also a powerful training tool. It allows you to give a good demonstration and then let participants practice doing what they have just learned and seen. It is still a very effective way to simulate a live call (sales, customer service, help desk). It works well because people can build on their learning: learn step one and practice, learn step two and practice steps one and two, learn step three and practice steps one, two, and three.

Important Benefits Of Role Playing Include:

- Repeated practice
- Immediate feedback
- Chance to correct behavior
- Incremental learning
- Can be repeated with many different skill and knowledge objectives
- Can learn without the stress of doing it on a live account call

Common Reasons to Use Role Plays

- Build interpersonal skills
- Improve communication
- Manager coaching
- Problem solving
- Increase sales or negotiation skills

Are there disadvantages to role play? I believe there are. Someone freezing in a role play or being embarrassed can have lasting effects on the individual, and the class can have a long memory of it. It doesn't just affect one person. Also, it isn't necessarily a good indicator of performance. There are instances when someone excels in performing a role play with peers, but isn't listening in front of a customer. And the reverse can be true. Someone can be nervous when role playing in a classroom situation, yet when they are in a familiar place on the job, they excel.

Role play remains a staple of training, particularly sales training, because it has the power to simulate the interaction that takes place on the job. However, it is exactly because of that power that role play can be so stressful. There is a continuum of stress in the various types of role play as shown below.

Stress Continuum

Low Stress
- Triads
- Other concurrent role play methods (like the Grinder, details later)

Moderate Stress
- Role play as a group (coaching and collaborating during the role play)

High Stress
- Role play in front of group
- In front of group with management present
- Recorded

Most people carry more anxiety in a traditional role play in classroom sessions than they do in a call on their toughest customer. Role playing in front of a class is like being under a microscope. Having management in attendance, and/or a camera, makes it worse.

Many companies are refusing the recording anymore. No one wants an old recording of a new salesperson—overpromising what a product can deliver—lying around in a  closet somewhere. Companies don't want any possibility that such recordings can end up in front of a judge. As a result, many pharmaceutical and insurance companies have already banned recording role plays.

However, many companies still record and conduct grueling new-hire training, because of legacy. Managers who went through stressful training and had to pass demanding tests, feel "if I had to do it, so should you." It becomes more of a test of character than training.

Or perhaps you have heard, "If they can handle the stress in front of the room, negotiating with a sales manager, then I know they can handle the stress with the customer." This is hazing, not training.

Suggestions for Taking the Stress Out

- Start with a series of grinder or group exercises and then graduate to triads. Because the stress level is lower, the focus will be on skill building.
- While triads are going on, notice reps who play their sales role very well. After they are done, in private, ask if they and their partner would be willing to demonstrate their sales call to the rest of the group. Chances are, they will gladly accept and will do well.
- Ask for other volunteers to demonstrate techniques they used or particular situations they were modeling.
- Always allow the "salespersons" to critique their performances first, followed by the "customers" and then any observers. Most sales reps are their own harshest critics.
- Give guidelines to the buyer and observer roles to ensure success and playing fair (no academy awards for toughest buyer).

The principles of adult learning say that the learning environment should be supportive, not stressful. The triad, grinder, and group role play techniques tend to be lower-stress role play versions, particularly when they are done "bedlam style" (everyone doing it at the same time, generating a lot of noise or bedlam). "Players" feel hidden by the noise of the whole group. For our purposes here, I am referring to these as role plays.

Key to reducing stress in role plays: never refer to the "R-word" (role play). Say we are going to practice what we have learned, or call it skill practice or application exercise.

Role play variation—triads. A triad works just the same as a large group role play but splits the participants into groups of three. One person is the buyer, one plays the role of the sales person, and one observes to give feedback. Or it could be the manager, the employee, and the observer. You can then have the groups switch roles so everyone has to participate. These small groups also allow for everyone to participate and observe in a shorter amount of time.

Role play variation— the Grinder. Despite its name, the grinder is another low-stress form of role play. I learned this method from SMT: Center for Sales Excellence (smt.org). People stand in two lines facing each other. One is the buyer and the other the seller, or one is the manager one the employee, or whatever combination of roles makes sense. They role play (generally for two minutes), buyers give one minute of feedback, and the sellers "grind" to the left (move to the next buyer, the person at the end of the line goes to the beginning). Now they are facing a different seller and they do it again. Feedback again. Grind again. Feedback again. Grind again. Switch roles and repeat three (or more) times. It is important to do a grinder activity at least three times (so participants can incorporate the feedback they get). One application is to use it for handling tough questions and giving each "buyer" a different question to ask. In this instance, the customer service or sales person role will get a chance to answer each question and get feedback on that answer.

Grinder Learnings Each Time
1. Get used to the process.
2. Get benefit from the feedback.
3. Incorporate new ideas for improvement.

When to Use the Grinder
- Overcoming objections
- Discussing the benefits of a product
- Introducing themselves or the company
- Practicing questioning
- Describing a new product release

I'll give you a tip from personal experience. Make sure you have the instructions really solid (practice with family, peers or neighborhood kids). This is hard for people to visualize from verbal instructions. So let them prepare (if required), get them in lines, verbally tell them what will happen, and then demonstrate it with a few people. This can be done with really large groups. It is tricky to manage (sometimes people need to stop in the middle of a conversation and move on to the next segment), it's loud and energizing. Try it, you'll like it!

Guidelines for a Successful Role Play

To make any type of role play successful you need to have a good scenario. Make it realistic and provide enough information to begin the discussion. Do not provide too much information or it may lead to a quick ending. Also, when running the role play, ensure all participants have a "play fair" mentality. Have a discussion on what is expected of the person playing the customer. The customer should not make the situation too difficult or too easy. Be careful, people get carried away, so the trainer must jump in when necessary.

SIMULATION

Generally, a simulation is simply a variation of a case study or role play, but the skill can be taught or applied through the use of technology. There are many ways to do a simulation, one is using a simulation product like Second Life or Avaya. Many business simulations use a board game technique to take you through the business financial process. Here are some Dos and Don'ts of e-learning simulations provided by Anders Gronstedt.

<u>Do:</u>
- Make it 3D immersive.
- Make it a game, with scores, high-scoring lists, levels, and badges.
- Launch the simulations with a big splash, play them at kick-off meetings, and advertise them in banners on the intranet and plugs in senior management communications.

<u>Don't:</u>
- Use 2D flatland webinars (WebEx, Adobe Connect, etc.), unless your goal is to treat insomnia.
- Focus the simulations on product presentation unless you want to turn your people into talking brochures; focus on asking the right probing questions and identifying customer needs.
- Be too serious about your training, use as much humor as your HR department allows.

But not all simulations need to involve technology. Taking sales people out of their territory and away from their customers has been a long time challenge. Steve Gielda solves this dilemma by bringing sales simulations to the classroom. This brings a high impact to the company by providing a higher level of knowledge transfer and application. According to Steve, there are four good reasons to consider classroom simulations:

- They create a realistic environment to test "what if" scenarios and provide the opportunity to make mistakes in a safe environment.
- They provide context, content, and process, which are relevant, realistic, and directly applicable on the job.
- They shorten learning cycles because of immediate feedback.
- They drive business impact through strategic application of critical selling skills.

So, what needs to be present for classroom simulations to succeed? They need to be:

- Fast-paced. Successful learning experiences must mimic the dynamic pace of the work environment.
- Feedback-rich. The experience must give people the opportunity to make mistakes and get expert feedback.
- Challenging and competitive. The program must represent challenging and competitive situations that engage people in the experience.
- Team-based. The best learning experiences should

be team-based so people can share best practices, push back on ideas, and strengthen one another's thinking.

- Relevant. Learning activities must be based on real world situations.
- Engaging and fun. The experience must create the motivation to learn

IMPROVISATION

One technique that is wonderful for practicing skills but is often overlooked, is the use of improv. People in many roles should be able to think on their feet and react quickly (facilitators, sales people, customer service). Practicing improvisation can improve this skill.

I had the pleasure of studying with Second City, the world-famous improvisation group. (Two of my teachers were Stephen Colbert and Steve Carell.) After completing their curriculum, and doing a number of shows, I saw many similarities between being successful improvising as an ensemble and being successful in business. People improvise every day, all the time. Trainers improvise every day, on every presentation. There are some fundamental improv principles that, if followed, could create more productive teams.

There is one caveat: Be careful about trying this at

home! Don't be afraid to ask for help from trained professionals! Improvisation is a skill, a muscle to be toned, just like presenting and facilitating. Some people aren't successful their first time facilitating a group. Improv demands a safe environment with people supporting each other. In the Resources section at the back of this book, I have included some basic and "safe" improv exercises that you will likely feel comfortable using in training situations.

The key: It's all in the debrief! Be sure to summarize what happened and the main take-aways from the exercise or activity. Tie it back to the business purpose.

Choose improv activities that support your objectives. The purpose for many exercises could be:
- Practice thinking on your feet
- Practice real listening
- Practice accepting what your teammate says, without judging

In most brainstorming or innovation sessions, people's roles should be neutralized. Every person's ideas are valued regardless of job level. And there are similarities to brainstorming in that ideas that seem impractical or out there can lead to the next big thing. Judgment and cognitive weeding out can come later! Early on, encourage ideas to flow. If you ask participants what the relevance was of this activity, they should be able to state it.

The facilitator should demonstrate and participate along with the group. Don't ask them to do things you are not willing to do. No one should be forced to do improv in front of a group. You can set up a safe environment and let people participate if they choose. If it is going on bedlam-style (several doing it simultaneously), it is generally safe.

This chapter has given ideas of how you can minimize lecture and build in interaction. As you incorporate some of the discussed methods, think about how you can get people out of their seats. Move to different tables, gather at a flip chart on the wall to brainstorm or do their exercise there. Encourage people to move around. Plan a reason to move to a different place in the room. The change of scenery is good, it is energizing to get up and move, and it restarts the attention span.

CHAPTER 4: WHAT'S NEXT?

Which Method to Use?

There is no one real answer to which method is the best to use for a given situation; it will vary based on content, participants, time, and instructor ability/style. The best approach is to be creative and try different methods. If you don't have access to the audience for some practice, grab a colleague or two and do a run-through. That will help ensure success when you do it the first time.

Remember to open your mind and be creative; there are places where it may be appropriate for a subject matter expert to share a lecture. Just think about how to support that with interaction to assist with learning transfer. When being creative, don't forget that all activities should support the course objectives. Don't just add an activity to add an activity. Be sure that it is appropriate, tied to the objectives, and that you understand why it is being used. And if you need to do a lecture in a traditional lecture style, make sure it is darn good!

Here is a simple test for knowing if you've chosen the right method: What if the VP or the CEO came into the room in the middle of a noisy exercise, a very competitive Jeopardy game, or when participants are tossing an invisible bowling ball around the room? Can you explain the learning value very concisely and convincingly? You should be able to articulate things such as:

- Before this activity they did X, which accomplished X objective. After this activity they can do X plus Y.
- This activity is stimulating creativity that we will apply to problem solving.
- The team is practicing listening to each other.
- This review game is reinforcing what they learned yesterday to improve retention.

 When choosing a method, the first question to answer is whether you are teaching knowledge or a skill. Knowledge is easier to learn because only content needs to be covered.

If you are teaching a skill, you actually need to teach or ensure knowledge first, then address teaching the skill. Remember to follow the three-step teaching model: (1) introduction to material, (2) guided practice, and (3) individual practice, incorporating activities for all three. You may first need a method to teach the knowledge and then continue with the application to make it a skill.

What Have We Learned?

Training events don't have to be all about lecture! There are many ways to engage learners and have fun during the first learning phase of introduction of material. There are successful training events that do not include any lecture at all in this first phase. Once the knowledge has been shared, practicing the skills and knowledge offers many opportunities to engage  learners in the learning process. Below are some of the things to keep in mind as you develop your fun, interactive and educational training programs.

<u>Keys for Interactive, Educational and Fun Programs</u>

- Seek activities that will nudge participants out of their comfort zones, but take it slow. Design one or two activities that will challenge the "norm" then evaluate how participants respond.

- An activity will solidify the learning for all learning styles.
- Interrupt extended activities with a break or a quick review of progress. Use the interruption to add variety and restart the attention span clock.
- To effectively address attention span, change both the style (vary facilitator location, delivery tools used, etc.) and the methodology (include activities, split into teams, etc.).
- People are capable; they learn new skills and achieve their goals every day. It's a mistake to sell them short in the classroom.
- To make your training more effective and engaging, use a variety of techniques to introduce learners to the material.
- Trust that your audience can lead learning and can do so without lectures.
- So often the success of many activities is in the debrief! Be sure to summarize what happened and the main take-aways from the exercise or activity. Your synopsis of the event helps solidify the learning in the minds of the participants.

A Few Parting Thoughts

I hope that in these examples and explanations you found legitimate business reasons to vary your training methodologies and design engaging methods in your training. There are certainly people who see training as serious business and see fun as something to be avoided in the classroom. I respect that there are different styles and that all can be effective. (I just happen to prefer engagement and a bit of fun!)

I have presented a number of tools and technique for your use during all three stages of the learning process. Be aware that simply because you have new tools doesn't mean they will immediately work well. Keep these tips in mind.

Tips for Adding Interactivity and Fun

- **Plan it**. The first time you want to try a new activity or method, plan it thoroughly. Practice it. Consider in advance the participants' styles, obstacles, or potholes that might come along.
- **Know your audience.** Choose activities that are a good fit and use variety.
- **Try it once with a test group** before you take it to your target audience. Your test run may be at home with neighborhood kids.

- **Do a run-through** with a couple of colleagues or people you trust. It is good to practice verbal instructions. It is good to see whether written instructions support the exercise. Where appropriate, have written as well as verbal instructions.
- **Don't do it to do it.** Don't do an exercise for the purpose of doing an exercise. Have a purpose; have a point. Make the connection so learners know why they are doing it. Better yet, let them explain why they just did it.
- **Let 'em fiddle**. Provide highlighters, Post-it notes, and tactile things to stimulate the senses. (Koosh balls, stress balls, or something for active bodies to handle) Having these items in a classroom to assist fidgeting participants helps them use some energy and other senses as they connect with content.
- **Allow some time**. Leave time in class (traditional or online) for participants to list ah-ha moments and link those to something they know. Reflection aids learning transfer.
- **Give rationale.** Let participants know why you are using different methodologies; remove the "curtain" so they can see that different methods help different people. People learn by seeing, hearing, and doing. We have all styles in the room, so we will teach using different methods to

respect each person in the group. You may find you don't like some of the methods, but it will likely be helping someone in the room.

It is my sincerest hope that there are a number of ideas here that you can try. Have fun with the Resources section which follows. It contains more ideas for activities to add interactivity, engagement and fun to your programs. Remember, just because I drink Tang doesn't make me an astronaut. Many of these approaches take planning and practice, not to mention that they need to be used in the right places, at the right time, for the right audiences.

CHAPTER 5: EXERCISE EXAMPLES AND INSTRUCTIONS

- Expert Panel
- Jury Trial
- Debate
- Card Game
- Timeline Activity
- Online Scavenger Hunt
- Case Studies
- Improv Examples
- Book Club
- Zoom!

EXPERT PANEL

Audience: Any size group; paired up.

Why use it: Present facts, listening, understanding issues.

Preparation:
- Give panel questions in advance. (Ask the audience to submit questions beforehand, if appropriate.)
- Have a moderator (required skills are intense listening and playing the role of "host;" moderator can be a lead panelist if needed).
- Prep the panel members as to what to expect (provide an agenda).

What to do:
1. Introduce the panel members mentioning their bios as they relate to the topics.
2. Moderator asks a question and then lets panel members answer the question.
3. Moderator asks the next question; panel members answer.
4. If there is disagreement or lively discussion, let members address concerns or ideas.
5. Take live questions from the group.
6. Moderator repeats the question, unless a microphone is used in the audience.
7. Moderator ends discussion with closing comments.

JURY TRIAL

Audience: Any size group. This can be done in person or in a synchronous online class.

Why use it: This is written for an American audience because it somewhat mirrors a US trial. Can be used to present facts and gain understanding of issues.

What to do:
- Assign roles: judge, bailiff, defense attorney, prosecution attorneys, witness for the defense, witness for the prosecution. The rest of the audience can be the jury.
- Give time for the attorneys to talk to their witnesses.

Execution (Sample script)
Bailiff: All rise. Court is now in session. Honorable Judge Susan presiding.

(The judge comes from outside the room wearing judge's robes (or black tablecloth) and/or white wig, looking serious or comical, holding a gavel.)

Judge: Welcome to the Court of Sales Professionals. This is the case of the questionable product. Bailiff, has the jury been impaneled?

Bailiff: Yes, your honor.

Judge: Who are they?

(Bailiff points to the jury, the whole audience or an identified couple of rows of people.)

Judge: Opening comments: The jury is going to hear statements from the defense on the advantages of The Good Guys product line, which is being challenged by the competition. Council for the prosecution is seeking the death penalty for Product Line X. Your job is to hear the testimony and decide on the merits of Product X for yourself. If you are convinced beyond a shadow of a doubt that Product X is guilty as charged, you are to find it guilty and recommend a sentence. If not convinced beyond a shadow of a doubt that Product X is a worthless product, you should enter a verdict of not guilty. Ladies and gentlemen of the jury: Do you understand your charge?

Sequence of events:
- Prosecution's opening comments
- Defense's opening comments
- Prosecution calls first witness
- Defense cross-examines
- Defense calls first witness
- Prosecution cross-examines
- Prosecution's closing arguments
- Defense's closing arguments

Judge: Closing comments: Ladies and gentlemen of the jury, the evidence has been presented on the legitimacy and value of Product X. Your job at this time is to render a verdict on the validity of this product. You are being asked to decide the guilt or innocence beyond a reasonable doubt. I am going to poll the jury at this time as to the guilt or innocence of this product. Jury, please raise your hand at this time if you agree with the prosecution and think that Product X should be put to death.

(Judge records hands.)

Those who feel not guilty?

(Judge records hands.)

The decision of the jury is final. Pound the gavel.

Notes/debrief: Be sure to debrief. Find out from the audience what salient points came out pro and con.

DEBATE

Here is a "not ready for prime time" debate method for training purposes. You will need three roles: moderator, proponent, opposition. The proponent and opposition can each be a team, if the topic and group dynamics lend themselves to this approach.

Audience: Any size group. This can be done in person or in a synchronous online class.

Why use it: Present facts, listening, accepting, supporting, understanding the issues.

What to do:
- Moderator reads debate issue
- Opening remarks from proponent in favor
- Opening remarks from opposition discussing why not in favor
- Opposition responds to the proponent points
- Proponent responds to the opponent
- Closing comments from each
- Conclusion is reached

Notes/Debrief: The conclusion can be done in one of several ways. You can have the audience vote on the conclusion, or the winning argument. You can have a panel of judges decide the outcome, and give their reasons why they chose the side they did. You can have a scripted conclusion which reviews the main points and reinforces the learning. Be sure to debrief to get participants' reactions.

Watch out: If there is a predetermined outcome, do not use this method. This method helps identify and bring out points from both sides. If there is a single, clearly right answer, choose a different method.

CARD GAME

How many ways can you split up a topic? How much can be learned by putting things back together again that have been split? "Shuffling a deck" of mixed items that were once together is a simple process and can reinforce lessons on processes or important combinations of elements. Here's how to do it.

Audience: Any size group, split up into teams of up to 6 people.

Why use it: Presenting facts, listening, accepting, supporting, understanding the issues.

What to do:
1. Determine the skills or knowledge area. Examples: a) Selling the benefits of Product X to customers with different needs b) Following a prescribed help ticket procedure in detail c) Matching feature, advantage, benefit.
2. Divide it into its component parts. Examples:
   a) Five different customers with five different sets of needs; 10 or 15 product benefits that could help each customer in appropriate combinations
   b) The ten-step call procedure and the many tasks that are to be accomplished in each call
3. Write all the component parts on card-shaped

sections of card stock. Print and cut.
4. Shuffle all the cards to mix them up.
5. Have participants sort them. Have a discussion about the various combinations.

Notes/Debrief:

- The project is best done in groups of four or five, where people can see all the cards laid out.
- In groups larger than five, you will need a set of cards for each small group.
- The main content of the lessons should be taught before the game. This is critical because the game is just one more way to teach complex subjects and cannot be a substitute for adequate instruction. Also, if the material is not understood before the game, the game will become extremely frustrating.
- There should always be a follow-up discussion at the end of the game. While challenging questions are good, there should be no ambiguity about the "right" answers, once you explain them.

TIMELINE ACTIVITY

Audience: Any size group divided into teams of up to 6 people.

Why use it: Present and organize facts.

What to do:
- Create flip charts with the decades as titles.
- Create note cards or Post Its - each one listing an event. Do not include the year with the description.
- Create one set of flip charts and one set of note cards for each group. This can also be done as one large group with only one set of flip charts and one set of note cards. Distribute the note cards among the group.

Example:
1950s
1951 Started making spaghetti sauce and pasta in mama's kitchen
1959 Started selling at the corner grocery store

1960s
1962 Gained first major account and sold in supermarkets
1967 Purchased a manufacturing facility and became Mama's Sauce and Pasta

1969 Created a marketing department; company slogan was "Just Like Mama Made"

1970s

1971 Acquired a noodle company and began the brand Noodles for Dinner

1975 Hired sales people and began national expansion

1980s

1985 Was in the top three brands in the US

1986 Company went public

1988 Introduced the Just Add Meat boxed dinners

1990s

1990 Expanded sales to Canada

1997 Brought the Allitalian brand to the United States

2000s

2004 Introduced a Pasta Fast entrée line

2001 Created the 10 Minute Meal Ideas promotion and website

ONLINE SCAVENGER HUNT

Audience: Small groups or individuals.

Why use it: Learn about an organization facts.

What to do:
Have participants find information from the company's intranet site, such as:
- Who is the VP of finance?
- What is the current stock price?
- How many SKUs are in the storage bag product line?
- What product lines are for sale in Canada?
- Where do you access the expense reporting?
- What is the phone number for customer service?
- How many regions does the company have?
- What is the order minimum for a printed deli storage bag?
- How do you order product brochures?

Notes/debrief: Review correct answers. Revisit anything difficult to find.

CORPORATE HEADQUARTERS SCAVENGER HUNT

Audience: Smaller groups.

Why use it: Learn information about an organization.

What to do:

This one is great for orientation to a new building. Possible tasks include:

- Get a cup from the cafeteria.
- Get a business card from customer service.
- Get a business card order form from the copy center.
- Determine your region number for expense reporting purposes.
- Bring a sales brochure for the newest product rollout.
- Get an autograph from someone in marketing.
- Get a company pen from the company store.
- Get a company envelope from the mail room.

Notes/debrief: Can tie this into a lunch hour. If the building is complex or confusing to get around in, include a tour. If not, allow people to ask questions or refer to a map to find their way.

CASE STUDY

Audience: Small groups or individuals.

Why use it: Learn about an organization's facts, problem solve, apply knowledge, synthesize info and apply to business scenario.

What to do:
In preparing case studies, consider these purposes:
- To allow participants to apply knowledge to a realistic situation
- To generate informed discussion around an issue
- Problem solving

Write down your learning objectives (what you want participants to get out of this exercise?). What do you need to create a case study?
- The case study formula
- The skills to be taught
- The industry/business vocabulary of the learners

To create your case study, follow these steps:
1. State the problem.
2. Select a setting that is not an exact replica of the work environment and characters who will not be recognized. You are trying to eliminate distractions or sidetracking.

3. Give sufficient background information to make an informed judgment.
4. Pose the problem as a question.
5. Write directions and discussion questions.
6. Write facilitator notes (what points are you trying to make).
7. Pilot and revise the case study (it can be just a few people who understand the audience, but don't present it to a live audience without testing it).

As your case study comes together, ask yourself these questions:

1 Is it too detailed?
2 Is there appropriate detail level and enough time?
3 Is anything distracting (sounds like my account, too close to industry)?
4 Is the dialogue clear?
5 Are directions clear?
6 Is the facilitator prepared?

Notes/Debrief: Discuss the team results or recommendations. Discuss why this solution was chosen. Discuss the team dynamics in this process.

Source: SMT: Center for Sales Excellence

IMPROV EXERCISES

Giving credit for improv games is always a tough thing. I have seen and done most of these, or a variation, at Second City. These exercises are chosen because of a relative low risk and high success factor.

Mirroring

Participants face each other and mirror the actions of their partner.

Audience: Any size group; paired up.

Why use it: Listening, accepting, supporting, team building, and concentration.

What to do:
- Have participants face one another. Ask partner A to begin a slow physical action (hand making a circle, head moving from side to side). Partner B should try to mirror (not anticipate) what partner A is doing. There is no verbal communication in this exercise.
- After a minute or so, ask the pairs to change who is leading and following sometime during the next 30 seconds (without verbally discussing the

handoff). Change the lead again with no signals. Facilitate working as a team, so observers can't tell who is leading and who is following and only the pair knows when the handoff happens.

- This activity may require a demonstration from the teacher! Make sure they understand that this activity is about seeing what your partner is doing, accepting that action, and mirroring the activity.
- This activity is about giving and receiving. The important thing is to have a balance and be able to lead or follow depending on the needs of the situation.

Debrief: What are keys to success here? (Having slow movements that your partner can follow. Not trying to trick the other person or make it hard to follow.) What can we learn from this exercise and apply to how we relate to each other in real life?

Sell This!

Audience: Small groups of 2 to 6 people.

Why do it: Creative thinking, listening and accepting peers' ideas, working together as a team.

What to do:
- Brainstorm a list (or come with a list prepared) of fictional product names and give one name to each small group.
- Give each group 15 minutes to come up with the following:
  - What the product is/does
  - A celebrity spokesperson for that product
  - A jingle or acting out a commercial

Each team presents their "product" to the large group. For example, "Our product is Can Can and it is a new motivational diet drink. Our celebrity spokesperson is Oprah Winfrey. Our jingle will be 'Maybe diets didn't work in the past, but now you Can Can.'"

Examples of fictional products are Bling-Bling, Orange Blast, Hidey Ho, Kookie, Cool Colors, Notables, Darl Doodles, Heat Up, Can Can, Alabaster, Lemon Zestier, Blue Laze. Or use terms that are meaningful to your industry. Fictional names should refer to something that doesn't exist.

Notes or debrief: Discuss how the team worked together. Were team members listening to each other? This doesn't have to be funny (although it often is). The point is for groups to work together and support each other's ideas.

Playing Catch

Audience: Any size; broken into groups of 6 to 10.

Why do it: Accepting, working together as a team, listening, adding energy.

What to do: The group will play catch with invisible balls.
- The facilitator tosses a "ball" to someone. They continue to play "catch" around the circle. Facilitator explains, we will continue to play catch, but it will get more complex.
- Start over. Toss a volleyball to someone and say "volleyball." The ball you toss should be the size of a volleyball. Have them continue to toss the ball and each time they toss it, they say "volleyball." Then toss a beach ball to someone else and say "beach ball." (Change the size of the ball you are throwing.) The group should continue tossing the beach ball and calling it by name. So now two different balls are being tossed around the circle at the same time. Add additional balls, things like footballs, tennis balls, and bowling balls. Watch the size and weight of the balls.
- If a ball gets lost, start over with one ball again.

The group is doing amazing if they can keep track of one ball for every two people (five different balls for ten people).

Notes or debrief: It is interesting to ask the group: What was the purpose of this exercise? What was the key to success here? Keys to success include: getting eye contact when you throw a ball to someone and stating clearly what ball it is, catching the same size and weight ball as being thrown, focusing with no distractions, throwing the ball to someone who is open, always throwing to the same person so he or she expects it.

BOOK CLUB

Audience: Groups of 6 to 10.

Why do it: Learn key concepts together, improve team dynamics, begin an organization culture initiative.

What to do: Read, review and discuss the book that all have read.
- Choose a book on a relevant business topic such as leadership or teamwork or something pertaining to the team.
- Assign the book as pre-reading and schedule an event to discuss.
- Create a discussion guide with questions for readers to review and gather thoughts on before meeting as a group.

Format: There are a variety of ways to do this. It can be a live class event, can kick off a larger session on the topic, a lunch and learn event where all participants bring a lunch and discuss the book over one or several lunch sessions, a virtual discussion via webinar or meeting or Google Hang Out.

Materials: Books, study guide, leader discussion questions.

Sample Study Guide

<u>Book Title:</u>
Author:

Purpose
Describe the purpose of the book club and any expectations for the group.

Overview
Describe any background information that may contribute to the discussion or context of the book chosen. (Why this book, why now?)

Reflection Question(s)
Include any reflection questions to consider before beginning or when finishing the book.

Using the book as a reference and your thoughts, answer the following questions.
List some key questions for discussion here. Provide space for thoughts.

Applying the Concepts to Your Job
Create questions to help draw out how this content would apply to the job.

Action Plan

Provide some prompting questions to help participants devise an action plan of incorporating key points.

Possible Leader's Questions:

- What is the biggest "ah-ha" that you received?
- Was it fun thinking about ....
- What can you do starting tomorrow to apply the concepts?

ZOOM!

Audience: 2 to 10 people.

Why do it? Participants work together to accomplish a task as a team.

Materials: Several copies of the book Zoom, by Istvan Banyai (1 for each team and one "solution").

Preparation: Cut out pages of the team books and put pages in random order. Keep one book intact as the "solution."

What to do?
- Give the random sequenced pages to each team. Provide verbal instruction to put the book in order.
- Let the team figure out what needs to be done.
- Once the team has the pages in the order they feel is right, give them the intact book to check their work.

Notes/debrief:
- The team needs to discuss and decide what to do, they often break into subgroups and sequence sections of the book.

- The book will generally be sequenced correctly, however they may get the front and back confused.
- Can be debriefed with "seeing from a different perspective." I use it for opening a training course where people may be asking, "Why am I here?"

UTOPIAN WRAP UP

Audience: Any size.

Why do it? Stimulate thinking on why to apply the course content. Wrap up a session

Materials: Flip chart page for each team

What to do?
Say: Let's fast forward. What happens when you leave here? Let's "picture utopia." Everyone imagine:
1. You have completed the training
2. You incorporate the learnings
3. The results are good

What will that look like? In small groups, give each team a flip chart and multiple colored markers.

The flipchart should be broken into quadrants, with the quadrants labeled:
- Me
- Manager
- Team
- Company

Ask each small group to draw "utopia" for each quadrant. We don't expect artists in the room and encourage stick figures! Or you can draw a word collage or word cloud or any visual representation of the concept.

- What will it look like for you?
- What will life be like for managers?
- What changes for the team?
- What changes for the company?

This is designed to be a light look, but make the point that the content in this course can really make an impact.

Notes/debrief:
Edit these quadrants as appropriate for the course topic. The groups can also write a description of what will change rather than drawing a picture.

ABOUT THE AUTHOR

Renie McClay is a global learning consultant who is passionate about connecting with people – from many cultures, on many topics and on many levels.

Renie has managed the training function for several Fortune 500 companies, including Kraft, Novartis, and Pactiv (makers of Hefty). After 20 years in corporate training and development roles, she started her own firm, Inspired Learning LLC. She designs and delivers training for increased performance.

Possessing a passion for travel, Renie has been to over 38 countries and enjoys getting to know new cultures. Her audiences have included people across the globe from Australia, Europe, Asia, Middle East, Latin America and North America. She facilitates in a classroom and virtually.

Renie is Adjunct Faculty for Roosevelt University and Concordia University. She also consults on a wide variety of sales and learning initiatives and is a facilitator for American Management Association. She is a Certified Professional of Learning and Performance (CPLP) and has a Masters in Global Talent Development from DePaul University. She is an honoree of the International Business Award and the Stevie Award for Women.

Connect!

Blog: www.inspiredtolearn.net/blog
Twitter: http://twitter.com/reniemcclay
LinkedIn: www.linkedin.com/in/reniemcclay
Facebook: www.facebook.com/reniemcclay
Website: www.inspiredtolearn.net
Email: info@inspiredtolearn.net

Other Books by Renie McClay:

10 Steps to Successful Teams (ASTD Press)
The Essential Guide to Training Global Audiences (Pfeiffer)
Fortify Your Sales Force: Leading and Training Exceptional Teams (Pfeiffer)

Many thanks to my rock star contributors:
Steve Gielda, BS, Ignite Selling
Anders Gronstedt, PhD., Gronstedt Group
Mike Rockelmann, M.ED, MBA, large US based
pharmaceutical company
Kimberly Seeger, MS, CPLP, Learniappe
Larry Straining, MBA, CPLP, Larry's Training
Trish Uhl, PMP, CPLP, Owl's Ledge LLC

And thanks to the talented and helpful Louann
Swedberg, Diane Boewe, and Vikas Sheth.

Other Books by Renie McClay:
10 Steps to Successful Teams (ASTD Press)
*Fortify Your Sales Force: Leading and Training Exceptional
Teams* (Pfeiffer)
The Essential Guide to Training Global Audiences
(Pfeiffer)

Made in the USA
Middletown, DE
06 September 2015